SANTA ANA PUBLIC LIBRARY

AR PTS: 0.5

SANTA ANA PUBLIC LIBRARY

Plateau Indians

Mir Tamim Ansary

Heinemann Library
Chicago, Illinois

Printed in Hong Kong
Designed by Depke Design

04 03 02 01 00
10 9 8 7 6 5 4 3 2 1

Library of Congress Cataloging-in-Publication Data
Ansary, Mir Tamim.
　　　Plateau Indians / Mir Tamim Ansary.
　　　　p. cm. – (Native Americans)
　　　Includes bibliographical references and index.
　　　Summary: An introduction to the history, dwellings, artwork,
religious beliefs, clothing, and food of the various Native American
tribes of the Plateau Region between the Cascades and the Rocky
Mountains.
　　　ISBN 1-57572-928-8 (library binding)
　　　1. Indians of North America-Northwest, Pacific Juvenile
literature. [1. Indians of North America-Northwest, Pacific.]
I. Title. II. Series: Ansary, Mir Tamim. Native Americans.
E78.N77A57　2000
9795'.00497–dc21

99-34897
CIP

Acknowledgments
The author and publishers are grateful to the following for permission to reproduce copyright material:
Cover: Marilyn Angel Wynn
Dr. D.E. Degginger, pp. 4, 9; The Bridgeman Art Library, p. 7; James Amos/National Geographic Image Collection, p. 8;
North Wind Pictures, pp. 10, 15, 17, 27; Washington State Historical Society, p. 11; National Anthropological Archives,
p. 12; Marilyn Angel Wynn, pp. 13, 18, 22; Edward Curtis/National Geographic Image Collection, p. 14; David
Boyer/National Geographic Image Collection, pp. 16, 29; Joel Sartore/National Geographic Image Collection, p. 19;
Edward Curtis/National Geographic Image Collection, p. 20; Willima Allard/National Geographic Image Collection,
p. 21; Sun Valley Video and Photography, p. 23; The Granger Collection, pp. 24, 26; Stock Montage, Inc., pp. 25, 30 top;
James Blair/National Geographic Image Collection, p. 28; AP/Wide World Photo, p. 30 bottom.

Every effort has been made to contact copyright holders of any material reproduced in this book. Any omissions will be
rectified in subsequent printings if notice is given to the publisher.

Our special thanks to Lana Grant, Native American MLS, for her
help in the preparation of this book.

Note to the Reader Some words are shown in bold, **like this.** You can find
out what they mean by looking in the glossary.

Contents

The Plateau Region

The Plateau is the region between the Cascades and the Rocky Mountains. From Oregon, it stretches north into Canada and east into Montana. The Columbia River flows in the southern part of the region. Canada's Frasier River flows in the north. Many other cold, fresh streams rush across this land.

The whole Plateau lies high above sea level. It is a region famous for its beauty and its great differences. Here you'll find dry deserts, mighty forests, snow-covered peaks, mountain meadows, and deep canyons. Elk and bighorn sheep roam among the rocks and trees. Salmon and **sturgeon** fill the waters.

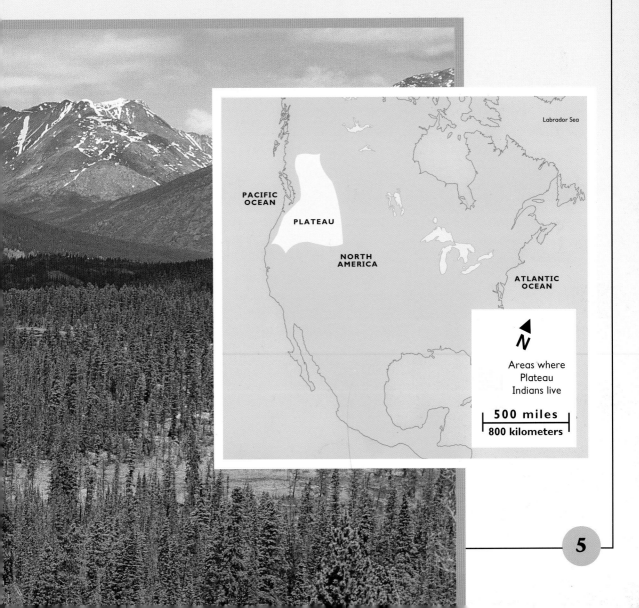

Labrador Sea

PACIFIC
OCEAN

PLATEAU

NORTH
AMERICA

ATLANTIC
OCEAN

N

Areas where
Plateau
Indians live

500 miles

800 kilometers

People Arrive

The first people of the Plateau came from Alaska at least 11,000 years ago. They moved south along the Cascades and then spread east. Later, other people moved north from the Great Basin. All these people settled in tiny villages. They built a way of life centered around the region's rivers.

PACIFIC
OCEAN

Kalispel
Spokane

Coeur d'Alene

Flathead

Walla Walla

Nez Perce

NORTH
AMERICA

N

Areas where
Plateau
Indians live

500 miles
800 kilometers

The tribes of the north spoke a group of languages called *Salishan*. Today we know these tribes by such names as the Kalispel, Coeur d'Alene, and Flathead. The tribes further south spoke languages of the *Sahaptian* group. These tribes included the Klickitat, the Walla Walla, and the Nez Perce.

Hudson Bay

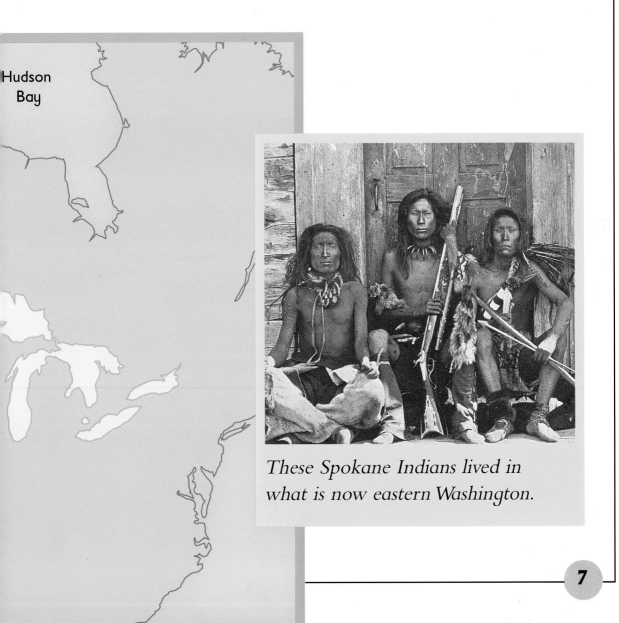

These Spokane Indians lived in what is now eastern Washington.

Foods of the Plateau

Salmon was the most important food of the Plateau. These fish live in the ocean, but they lay their eggs in rivers, far upstream. The Indians built wooden platforms next to big falls. From these, they netted, hooked, or speared the fish. Salmon was dried, **smoked,** or eaten fresh.

This Indian fisherman from Warm Springs, Oregon, is catching salmon with a net.

Camas bulbs were an important trade good for the Klamath Indians.

Plateau Indians gathered wild plants, too. The Klamath of southern Oregon ate camas lily bulbs. They steamed the bulbs for days in pits in the ground. Another important food was kouse, or biscuit root. This root was boiled, mashed, and formed into bricks. The bricks were baked into a kind of bread.

Shelters North and South

Northern tribes, such as the Thompson, lived in earth **lodges.** These homes were partly underground. A dome of poles was built over a pit some six feet (two meters) deep. The dome was topped with grass and earth. The door was in the roof. People climbed down ladders into their homes.

An earth lodge could be as much as 30 feet (9 meters) across.

The walls of this Yakima lodge are woven of bulrushes, a kind of plant.

In the south, many people lived in cone-shaped lodges. **Cattail** mats were wrapped around a frame of poles. The Nez Perce sometimes built "longhouses" for summer gatherings. These could be 15 feet (5 meters) wide and over 150 feet (46 meters) long. Thirty families often lived in one longhouse!

Clothes of Leather

Early people of the Plateau made clothes out of bark and other plant parts. Later, they began to use **tanned** antelope, elk, or deer hides instead. Men usually wore leggings, a **breechcloth,** and a shirt or robe. They plucked their beards and sometimes painted their faces, too.

This Nez Perce boy is wearing a shirt decorated with weasel skins.

The yoke or collar of a woman's dress was often a beautiful work of art.

Women wore long dresses over their leggings. A woman's dress usually came down to her ankles. The top was folded over to make a very large collar, or "yoke." This yoke was decorated with fringes, beads, and porcupine quills. Each tribe had its own style of yoke.

River Traders

Rivers were the best way to travel in this region. Every tribe, therefore, made boats or canoes. Canoe styles differed, however. The Kalispel, for example, made square-tipped canoes. Thompson craftworkers made canoes that had a sharp point at each end. Some tribes rolled reed mats into bundles and tied them together to make big rafts.

Canoes like this one were usually made of cedar bark.

These Native Americans are trading goods at the store in a trading post.

Most tribes depended on trade to fill many of their needs. Traders gathered each fall at big centers such as The Dalles, on the Columbia River. Traders came from as far away as California and Montana. Each tribe made or gathered something special to trade at these fairs.

Coming of Age

Teenagers went through hard training to become adults. Girls lived alone for months. They took sweat baths to become strong. Older women taught them how to behave as adults. During this time, a girl hoped to get a **guardian spirit**—a magical being who would protect her throughout life.

A girl's guardian spirit sometimes gave her the power to become a healer or shaman.

A boy on a vision quest might spend days in a spot like this, waiting for his guardian spirit to appear.

Boys found guardian spirits on vision quests. A vision quest was a journey to a lonely spot. The boy stayed there alone, without food, water, or weapons. His guardian spirit might appear in the form of an animal. Indians of the Plateau still honor many of these customs and beliefs.

Festivals and Myths

Each year, a few young people get their first **guardian spirits**. They announce their news at the winter Spirit Dance. This festival lasts several days and ends with an exciting dance. Here, young adults sing their special songs—songs they have learned from their guardian spirits

This young Nez Perce man is dressed for a celebration.

This dancer is acting out a story about the trickster Coyote, hero of many Plateau myths.

Many Plateau tribes tell a similar story about the world. They say only animals lived here at first. A terrible giant ruled them. The hero, Coyote, killed the monster and cut him into pieces. Each piece became a tribe. Most tribes said they were born from the giant's heart.

Spanish Horses

In the 1500s, the Spanish brought horses to America. Comanche Indians got horses by raiding ranches in New Mexico. The Shoshone got them from the Comanche. Soon all the Plateau Indian tribes had these animals. Horses brought important and sudden changes to their way of life.

Indians of the Plateau quickly made horses part of their way of life.

Appaloosas were unusually tough and sure-footed ponies bred by the Nez Perce.

The Nez Perce became expert horse **breeders.** They bred the famous Appaloosa, a strong, spotted horse. They liked to dress up their horses and even paint them. For this reason, they liked white horses best. By the 1850s, it was not unusual for one Nez Perce family to own 1,500 horses.

A Changing World

Horses replaced canoes in the Plateau. Using horses, people could move fast and far in any direction. They traveled to the Great Plains to hunt buffalo. They raided the Plains people—but traded with them, too. The Plains Indians wanted such goods as salmon oil, eagle feathers, and bows made from mountain sheep horns.

Once they got horses, the Nez Perce traveled hundred of miles to trade and hunt.

Feather headdress like this were valuable trade items.

The Plateau tribes wanted pipes, skins, and special clothes made on the Plains. They liked the deerskin robes made by the Crow Indians. They placed high value on the feather **headdresses** made by the Sioux. Trade with the Plains changed clothing styles of the Plateau tribes.

White Settlers Arrive

By the mid 1800s, White settlers began pouring into **"Oregon Territory."** Many Indians felt crowded by them. Trouble broke out. To prevent war, the U.S. government gave lands called **reservations** to many tribes. The Indians were supposed to own these lands. But in 1860, gold was found on the Nez Perce reservation.

Over 10,000 White settlers moved into Oregon by 1840.

Chief Joseph is considered one of the greatest of Native American leaders.

The U.S. government told the Nez Perce to move to Idaho so that White miners could search for gold. Some groups of Nez Perce were slow to obey. The U.S. Army moved in to punish them. One band decided to move to Canada where they would be safe. Their leader was a man named Chief Joseph. Other Nez Perce soon joined him.

The Nez Perce War

The Nez Perce traveled 1,400 miles (2,253 kilometers) in 4 months to get to Canada. The army chased them all the way. Many times the Nez Perce looked like they were trapped, but they escaped. They out-fought the army in eighteen important battles. But at last, on October 5, 1877—just 40 miles (64 kilometers) from Canada, the U.S. Army caught the brave Nez Perce.

Chief Joseph and his tired people gave up after a five-day battle.

Many Nez Perce were killed. Chief Joseph **surrendered** to the army. The Nez Perce were sent to Kansas and Oklahoma, where many died of disease. In 1885, the survivors were allowed to return to the Plateau. But none ever returned to the Wallowa Valley, Chief Joseph's homeland.

The 20ᵗʰ Century

In 1941, the Grand Coulee Dam was built across the Columbia River. Today, it is one of ten dams across this mighty river. These dams hold water that farmers use to water crops. The dams also make electricity. But the dams have flooded much land. These were areas that Indian tribes once called home.

The Grand Coulee Dam flooded many lands once held by Native Americans.

28

Kah-nee-Tah is a popular Indian resort east of Mt. Hood.

Groups of tribes now share **reservations**
from Washington to Wyoming. Some of these
"**consolidated** tribes" run successful businesses.
In Oregon, for example, the Warm Springs
Reservation welcomes visitors to Kah-Nee-Tah, a
modern hotel. Money from these businesses pays for
schools, health care, and other tribal needs.

Famous Plateau Indians

Sacajawea (Lemhi Shoshone, 1785?–?) joined the Lewis and Clark expedition in 1805. She traveled with them across the Rocky Mountains to the Pacific Ocean. Since she spoke both English and Shoshone, she helped the explorers talk with Indians they met along the way.

Christine Quintasket (Salishan, 1884?–1936) Quintasket made her living as a farmworker, but she wrote stories at night. In 1927, she published her novel *Cogewa* under the pen name Mourning Dove. She was the first woman elected to the Colville Tribal Council.

Dan George (Suquamish, 1899–1977) was a chief of the Salish nation and a busy movie actor. He played Old Lodge Skins in the movie *Little Big Man.* He was nominated for an Academy Award for that role. In 1970, he won a Best Actor award from the New York Film Critics Circle.

Glossary

breechcloth piece of cloth worn around the hips and through the legs

breeder person who raises one type of animal

cattail type of reed with a fuzzy top that looks like a cat's tail

consolidated joined together

guardian person who protects someone or something

headdress special hat

lodge small house, such as a cabin or hut

Oregon Territory area created in 1848 that included the present states of Idaho, Oregon, and Washington, and parts of Montana and Wyoming

reservation area of land set aside for Native Americans

smoked food that has been cooked by letting smoke pass over it for a long time

spirit being that has life but cannot be seen, often having special powers

sturgeon large fish with a long snout and rows of hard plates on the skin

surrendered gave up

tanned to have turned an animal hide into leather by soaking it in special liquids

More Books to Read

Osinski, Alice. *The Nez Perce.* Danbury, Conn.: Children's Press, 1988.

Troy, Don. *Chief Joseph.* Chanhassen, Minn.: Child's World, 1998.

Shaughnessy, Diane, and Jack Carpenter. *Sacajawea: Shoshone Trailblazer.* New York: Rosen Publishing Group, 1997.

Index